ELAINE LANDAU

THE ABENAKI

Franklin Watts   A Division of Grolier Publishing
New York   London   Hong Kong   Sydney   Danbury, Connecticut
A First Book

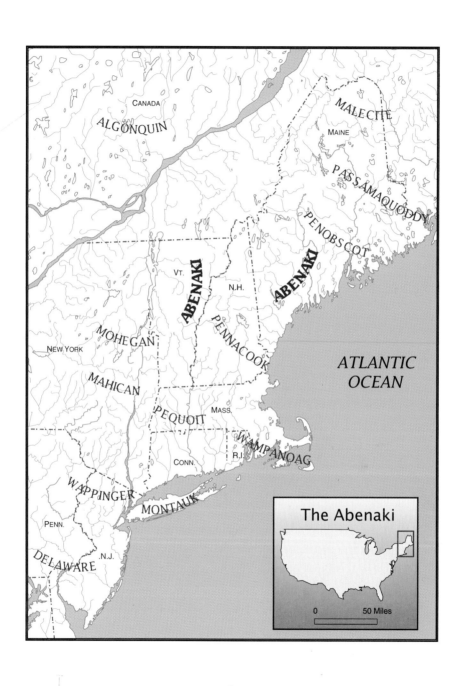

CANADA

ALGONQUIN

MALECITE

MAINE

PASSAMAQUODDY

PENOBSCOT

ABENAKI

VT.

N.H.

ABENAKI

PENNACOOK

MOHEGAN

NEW YORK

MAHICAN

ATLANTIC OCEAN

PEQUOIT

MASS.

CONN.

R.I.

WAMPANOAG

WAPPINGER

MONTAUK

PENN.

.N.J.

DELAWARE

The Abenaki

0   50 Miles

THE ABENAKI

In the early seventeenth century, many American Indian children in what is now the northeastern United States were told about Azeban, "the Raccoon." Azeban was a trickster whose mischievousness and curiosity often landed him in a good deal of trouble.

In one such tale, Azeban walked to the edge of a cliff just above a magnificent waterfall. At first he rested there, enjoying the sound of the swiftly moving water below. But then he thought that perhaps he could make even more noise than the rushing rapids. So Azeban began to shout. He shouted so hard and so loud that he lost his balance and fell off the cliff. To his embarrassment, he was roughly tossed over the waterfall that he had hoped to be mightier than.

Young people heard many different stories about Azeban. Like the other tales passed down to them, these stories had a dual purpose. They were meant both to amuse the children and to teach them important lessons about survival and the ways of their people. In this tale, excessive pride and failing to respect nature resulted in Azeban's downfall. It's a story typical of those told by the Abenaki, a group of American Indians sometimes called the "dawnland people" or "the ones from where the sun comes [the East]."

The Abenaki are frequently described as comprising two groups, known as the Eastern Abenaki and Western Abenaki. Before the arrival of Europeans in the North America, the Western Abenaki inhabited what is presently New Hampshire, Vermont, and parts of Ontario and Quebec in what is today called Canada. Eastern Abenaki villages were largely in Maine. The various bands, or subdivisions, of the Eastern and Western Abenaki are often known by their geographical locations. These Indians include the Missisquois, Penacooks, Pigwackets, Arosaguntacooks, Kennebecs, and Penobscots. The Eastern and Western Abenaki along with several other American Indian tribes in the region, are collectively known as Wabanaki, which is their name for themselves.

There are some dialect (language) and cultural differences among various Abenaki bands (groups). Yet, through the years, they have allied themselves with one another for various reasons, and in many ways are more alike than different. This is the story of these early Northeasterners before and after their contact with the white people.

ABENAKI VILLAGES AND MOVEMENT

The Abenaki built their villages along the region's rivers. These waterways were crucial to their survival, providing a readily available means of canoe transportation as well as a vital source of food and water.

Abenaki villages were usually made up of a number of long rectangular birch-bark or log houses, large enough for several related families to live in. The dwellings had arched roofs with openings to allow smoke from the hearths within to escape. In some communities, the houses were spread along the river rather than built next to one another. This left the Indians with little protection against enemy attacks. So in these locations the Abenaki constructed fortlike structures on steep cliffs above the water, to which they could retreat for safety.

THE INSIDE OF AN ABENAKI BIRCHBARK HOUSE
MIGHT HAVE LOOKED LIKE THIS. NOTICE THE
ANIMAL SKINS USED FOR WARMTH AND COMFORT.

When away from their villages for extended periods, the Abenaki used portable homes that they could take from place to place. These wigwams, as they were called, were shaped like upside down ice cream cones. Made from either animal skins or birch-bark sheets, the temporary dwellings were held up by poles.

Most wigwams had two deerskin-covered openings. One of these "doors" was usually left open to rid the house of excess smoke from the fire used for warmth and cooking. These structures could be adjusted, however, to suit the weather conditions at different times of the year. In the winter, a wigwam might be tightly sealed to keep out the snow and cold. But during the summer months, both doors were left open to allow a cool breeze to enter.

Abenaki villages varied in size. Those located at excellent fishing sites on central rivers tended to be larger than those on less important waterways. While exact figures are not available, it's estimated that between five hundred and fifteen hundred people inhabited these communities.

At various times of the year, many Abenaki left their villages. When the main hunting season began in late February, usually only the elderly and the ill remained at home. The others headed for hunting territory where game was plentiful.

WIGWAMS MADE EXCELLENT TEMPORARY HOMES. THEY
COULD BE TAKEN APART QUICKLY AND PUT BACK UP WHEN
THE INDIANS REACHED THEIR NEXT DESTINATION.

The various hunting areas were clearly defined by their physical features. Each contained a tributary stream leading to a larger river. This allowed a hunter to reach any part of the territory by canoe. When the rivers froze, Abenaki hunters either walked on ice or followed nearby trails to reach their destination.

Once the weather became warmer, Abenaki returned to their village for the spring fishing season. Often the villages were near some of the best fishing rapids. This was helpful to Abenaki fishermen who would stand in the rapids with nets and fishing spears. During the spring, crops were also planted near the villages, to be harvested in late summer or early fall.

In the summer, some people remained in the village but others moved to temporary camps near the ocean or on the shores of nearby lakes, streams, and ponds. It was cooler there, and the flies and mosquitoes seemed less bothersome. Abenaki enjoyed good lake fishing from dugout canoes purposely left at these sites. Some fished during the day, but others lit torches and went out on the lakes after dark. The Indians believed that firelight attracted more fish. Besides these fishing trips, the Abenaki also took longer journeys during the summer. Some visited or traded with other American Indians who lived a distance away.

A TRAIL IN
ABENAKI
HUNTING
TERRITORY

But by fall, all the travelers returned. The small
family bands prepared to leave for their hunting terri-
tories for the second time that year. This was essential
to amply stock their food supply.

At the onset of the freezing winter, everyone
returned to their villages for a brief period. Then fol-
lowing the midwinter feast, the Indians once again
began the yearly cycle of movement that helped
ensure their people's survival.

FOOD

The Abenaki's food came directly from the land and the bodies of water surrounding them. With their villages so near the water, fish was an important part of their diet. The catch varied somewhat with the village's location. Shellfish was a staple for Eastern Abenaki on the coast of Maine. When the tide was low, men speared crabs and lobsters from their canoes. Clams were plentiful as well. They also fished these cold coastal waters for salmon, eels, shad, smelts, and other fish.

Western Abenaki were superior fishermen as well. At times, they caught more fish than they could eat. Then the Indians *smoked* what was left and stored it away for winter.

Hunting animals brought the Abenaki still another food source. Eastern Abenaki men hunted harbor seals, porpoises, and various types of *waterfowl*. In the winter, both Eastern and Western Abenaki scouted their hunting territory for moose, bear, and deer. They carried their bows and arrows, long lances, and knives with them as they traveled through the forest stalking game. The Abenaki were especially skilled at moose calling and used this technique to draw these animals to them. They also laid traps for smaller animals such as muskrats, otters, and beavers.

Once an animal was caught, the Abenaki were careful about how they used it. If they killed a waterbird or beaver, they did not merely discard its bones after cleaning and preparing the animal. Instead, the bones were returned to the water with a prayer that these animals continue to thrive. Avoiding waste, the Indians used nearly every part of a slain animal. They believed that if proper respect wasn't shown to these creatures, the animals would no longer let themselves be caught.

Specific hunting areas were used by particular family groups. The only others allowed to hunt or even walk through that area were relatives of the family. These Indians also carefully managed their hunting regions to ensure a continuing supply of game. Only a portion of these areas were hunted at any one time. This allowed the animals to reproduce in the

ABENAKI WERE SKILLED HUNTERS. IN SOME AREAS,
WATER FOWL (ABOVE) AND OTTERS (BELOW) WERE
IMPORTANT TO THE INDIANS' FOOD SUPPLY.

sections previously used. If there was an abundance of game, the extra meat was left to freeze in wooden troughs. When food later became scarce, it would be thawed out and cooked.

While Abenaki men hunted and fished, the women gathered an assortment of foods for their families. Sometimes they sung special gathering songs as they worked. These females collected beechnuts, butternuts, and hickory nuts. During the summers they picked a variety of fruits and berries that might be eaten fresh, cooked, or baked in breads. Left over nuts and berries were dried and put away for future use. Various wild plants and greens were collected by the women as well. The ground nut, a wild plant very much like a potato, was an important part of the Eastern Abenaki's diet.

Just as nearly every part of a slain animal was used, the Abenaki never wasted the plants they picked. For example, the sprouts of most wild edible plants were either eaten raw or made into a flour to be used later. The plant's seeds and blossoms were also eaten while the stems might be cut and woven into mats or bedding. The women gathered medicinal plants for healing towards the end of summer, as the Abenaki believed these plants were most powerful then. They would pound them into powders to treat various illnesses.

YARROW (SEEN HERE) AND OTHER PLANTS WERE USED
BY THE ABENAKI FOR HEALING PURPOSES.

CORN AND SQUASH WERE AMONG THE CROPS
GROWN BY THE ABENAKI FOR HEALING PURPOSES.

Abenaki women and children also tapped maple trees for syrup. To do this they slashed the tree trunks and inserted hollow twigs for the sap to flow through. The thick liquid would slowly drip into buckets that the women placed beneath the twigs. After it was collected and boiled, the sap was ready to use in food preparation.

The Abenaki grew crops to bolster their food supply as well. Abenaki women planted corn, beans, and squash on small plots near their villages. Tobacco was the only crop cultivated by the men. While food crops supplemented their diet, the Indians couldn't always depend on these harvests. At any time, poor soil or weather conditions could result in crop failure.

FAMILY LIFE AND CUSTOMS

The family was the basis of Abenaki society. Each Abenaki was born into a household generally made up of a father, mother, and siblings (brothers or sisters). Usually several of these related families shared a large dwelling. Even though they all occupied the same house, each family had its own fire and living space.

When a young Western Abenaki couple married, most often they moved into the groom's family home. If the bride's family had significantly more wealth and status within the village, however, the new couple would establish their own fire in the family of the bride's home. In cases where there simply wasn't room with either the bride's or groom's family, the new couple would built a small house of their own near either family. Among Eastern Abenaki newlyweds tended to live with the bride's family.

Every extended family was associated with a particular animal. The Eastern Abenaki believed their families were descended from that animal. Western Abenaki families were usually represented by animals that were especially prevelant in their hunting areas. A particular animal might have also been chosen because it was thought to be characteristic of the family. Therefore, as bears were believed to be especially shrewd and resourceful, members of the Abenaki bear family liked to think of themselves as that way as well. Various animal symbols or totems representing Abenaki extended families included the turtle, bear, fish, raccoon, and hummingbird, among others.

The Abenaki highly valued their children. As a quiet and reserved people, they rarely raised their voices to scold them. Instead, the Abenaki generally disciplined and educated their offspring by continually repeating tribal tales with strong moral messages. Knowing that children watch and copy their elders, these American Indian parents tried to set a good example as well.

When, despite these measures, children misbehaved, they were taken aside and spoken to. In severe

AN ABENAKI TURTLE CARVING: ABENAKI FAMILIES
BELIEVED THEY SHARED A SPECIAL BOND WITH THE
ANIMALS THEY WERE LINKED TO.

cases, a young person's face might be blackened while the child was made to stand outside his or her home for a time. Under no circumstances, however, were Abenaki children beaten.

Usually, Abenaki offspring were primarily reared by their grandparents or aunts and uncles. Their instruction in the skills they needed began early. Abenaki boys learned to hunt, fish, build houses and canoes, and fashion bows, arrows, knives, and spears. Young males began practicing with a bow and arrows when they were just five or six years old. At ten or twelve, they were ready to hunt with the older men in their families.

Young Abenaki girls were schooled in the ways of their people as well. They learned to care for infants and children by helping the older women with these tasks. Girls were taught to plant and harvest crops, properly cook food, and to gather, dry, and store the wild fruits, greens, and nuts their people depended on. They also learned to make clothing and various household items.

Marriage proposals from young Abenaki males were usually made through a go-between who would bring gifts from the hopeful groom. If the girl refused to marry him, the presents were returned. But if she and her family agreed, the couple began a trial period

THE ABENAKI MADE GOURD RATTLES AND MOOSE
HIDE DRUMS. THESE DRUMS WERE USED DURING
SOME CELEBRATIONS.

of living together. During this time, however, the young couple were strictly chaperoned and did not live as husband and wife. If they decided that they didn't want to spend the rest of their lives together, the would-be bride and groom parted. But by then the young man was not permitted to take back his gifts.

Just as marriage required certain rituals, there were specific rites surrounding death. The Abenaki believed it was essential for a dead person to be buried. If they were not, the living feared that the deceased's spirit would hover over the corpse and their village. During the winter, however, when the ground was frozen solid, that wasn't always possible. Therefore in such instances, bodies were placed on a high scaffold until the earth thawed in early spring. It was important that the corpse be elevated to protect it from hungry animals. If a man died while off hunting, his companions would build the scaffold for the body. It then became the responsibility of the first person who found him that spring to bury the body.

People who died in their villages were laid to rest in their most elaborate clothes. Rather than being placed in coffins, bodies were wrapped in a roll of bark tied with a cord. Abenaki were buried with sufficient food to see them through their journey to the next world. Tools, weapons, and utensils were also placed in the grave for the deceased.

After the burial, a wooden tent-shaped structure was built over the grave. This marked the grave site as well as identified the dead person. When a Western Abenaki chief died an oval ring of trees was planted around his grave.

At Abenaki funerals, those closest to the deceased openly mourned. A woman whose husband died could not remarry or attend tribal festivals for a year. Such women showed they were in mourning by wearing a hood on their heads. The custom was similar for men whose wives dies. They did not participate in village sporting events or celebrations throughout the year.

However, the Abenaki believed that the deepest sorrow resulted from the loss of a child. A dead child's mother might express her grief by cutting off her hair and blackening her face. Friends and relatives would bring the mourning parents presents hoping to ease their pain. In return for the sympathy and kindness shown them, the parents were expected to give a feast.

CLOTHING AND UTENSILS

Before Europeans arrived in North America, the Abenaki made nearly everything they needed from raw materials in their environment. The men relied on wood, stone, and animal bones and sinews to create bows, arrows, knives, and spears for hunting and fishing.

Abenaki males made canoes out of white birch-tree bark. This enabled them to take their families, gear, and dogs to various areas of their hunting territory by water. These lightweight crafts were durable, easy to carry, and worked well even in shallow streams.

After the hunt, sturdy moose-hide canoes might be built to transport the slain animals to their villages. Once the Abenaki arrived, the canoes were taken apart and the moose-hide was used to make other

BESIDES BIRCHBARK AND MOOSE-HIDE CANOES,
THE ABENAKI CREATED DUG-OUT CANOES SUCH
AS THE ONE SHOWN HERE. THESE VESSELS WERE
MADE OUT OF HOLLOW LOGS.

THE INSIDE OF AN ABENAKI BASKET: MANY SUCH MODERN DAY BASKETS FEATURE MULTI-COLORED BANDS.

items. In keeping with Abenaki custom, meat from the season's first kill would be shared with other villagers.

Eastern Abenaki women made wide-mouth pottery jugs for cooking, carrying, and storage. Sometimes they decorated their pottery with shells or designs created by pressing pieces of cord into the damp clay. The

THESE BEAUTIFULLY DECORATED
MOCCASINS REFLECT THE SKILL OF
ABENAKI CRAFTPERSONS.

baskets that they created from strips of bark or wood were useful containers as well.

Abenaki women also made their family's wardrobe, which varied according to the season. In the warmer months, Abenaki men wore a belt and *breech-clout*—a piece of tanned animal skin tied around their hips and thighs. Women also used belts and breech-clouts, but wore knee-length buckskin skirts and long blouses over them. Moose-hide moccasins were worn throughout the year. But in the winter the Indians layered their footwear. They wrapped a piece of rabbit fur or animal skin around their feet before putting on the moccasins. Then they placed a high-cut outer shoe over their moccasins as well.

To keep warm, both Abenaki men and women wore thigh-high leggings and either robes of beaver fur or coats with moose-hide panels. While these outer garments were sleeveless, separate sleeves could be added when it was cold. The Abenaki usually didn't wear hats but hunters sometimes used moose-hide caps or a buck's-head hat with the antlers still attached.

RELIGION

The Abenaki's religion cannot be separated from their view of the world and everyday life. Like all American Indians, the Abenaki respected nature and believed that the environment was alive and powerful in unique ways. This meant that rocks, trees, grains of sand, and blades of grass were living things just like animals and people. The Abenaki felt that they existed on earth as part of the natural scheme of things.

Young Abenaki men went on *vision quests* to seek their guardian spirits. A person's guardian spirit was thought to shield that individual from danger and harm. Before embarking on a vision quest, the young man would *fast* for several days to purify his mind and body. Then he would go off alone to an isolated place and remain there until his guardian spirit came to him in a vision or dream. A guardian spirit could take many forms—it could appear as a bear, hawk, deer, or something entirely different.

NOTE THE LARGE ROCK IN THE WATER. THIS
SACRED SPOT IS WHERE ODZIHOZO IS BELIEVED
TO HAVE TURNED HIMSELF TO STONE.

Before beginning a vision quest, the young man might consult with a *shaman*. A shaman was an individual whom the Abenaki believed was born with special spiritual powers to cure the sick, locate game, or even see into the future. Shaman usually commanded a great deal of respect in their villages.

Western Abenaki believe that all living things were created by a great power known as Tabaldak, or "the Owner." Tabaldak is said to have made the first man and woman on earth out of stone. Not being pleased with his work, however, he tried again. This time he made a man and woman of wood and was delighted with the results. The Western Abenaki believe that the wooden couple were the start of the Indian people from whom they descended.

Odzihozo was thought to be another extremely powerful being who created himself from the dust shaken off by Tabaldak. Odzihozo was determined to reshape the world to his own liking. He fashioned mountains out of dirt piles and molded ravines and channels that turned into springs and waterways. It's said that Odzihozo's favorite creation was a Vermont and New York lake now known as Lake Champlain. Western Abenaki believe that one day Odzihozo simply sat down on a large rock in Lake Champlain and turned himself to stone. That way he could enjoy the lake's beauty and peacefulness forever. Today the spot is still regarded as sacred by the Indians.

ABENAKI CHIEFS

Abenaki daily life was never strictly regulated by a chief or governing body. Because many of those living in the same village were related, family pressure and a sense of duty to one another encouraged proper behavior. Yet even within this somewhat flexible structure, there were both family leaders and village chiefs.

The various family elders composed the village governing council. One of these elders served as the group's civil chief presiding over the council. The civil chief was also the group's representative at meetings with other Abenaki or with other Indians from surrounding areas. Usually this person, known as the sagamore, was highly respected within the community and a good provider.

A civil chief was expected to be wise, as well as patient and generous in his dealings with others. He remained in office for life unless removed for improper conduct. Sagamores were among the few Abenaki men who sometimes had more than one wife. Large families were often helpful to these chiefs in carrying

PRESENT-DAY ABENAKI LEADERS MAY
MEET AT TRIBAL COUNCIL BUILDINGS
SUCH AS THIS ONE TO DISCUSS ISSUES
AFFECTING THEIR PEOPLE.

out their social and counseling responsibilities within
their villages.

Being a civil chief was not easy. Because he did not
have absolute authority, the civil chief lacked the power
to make the others do as he wished. Therefore, Abenaki
civil chiefs had to depend largely on their personal per-
suasiveness in achieving goals. As might be expected,
some civil chiefs wielded greater influence in their com-

munities than others. Besides its civil chief, each Abenaki village also had a war chief. Like the civil chief, a war chief had considerable prestige in his community. War chiefs, however, were usually selected as a result of their bravery and valor in battle.

The war chief sprung into action when the group faced a conflict. At the start of hostilities, he would ceremoniously stand up with a red club in his hand and ask for volunteers. Other Abenaki known as war leaders also rose and asked for men to fight alongside them. Each war leader would lead a group of ten Abenaki into battle.

Once the various war parties were formed, the men feasted and danced into the night. Before the battle, they would put red paint on their faces and draw pictures of their past battle feats on their bodies. This prevented them from being mistaken for the enemy by other Abenaki fighters.

Prior to the arrival of Europeans, Western Abenaki were more often involved in conflicts than the Eastern groups. While the Western Abenaki were not particularly warlike, they frequently had to defend themselves against attacks from their aggressive neighbors, the Iroquois. Yet these flare-ups among Indian neighbors would seem minor once the flood of settlers to the area began. From then on, the lives of the Abenaki would be changed in ways they never imagined possible.

THE WHITE INVASION

Early Abenaki contact with whites came largely from explorers and traders who arrived on Indian land. Furs from the animals hunted by the Abenaki, were a highly desired item in Europe. Nobles and wealthy merchants living in drafty castles and manor houses sought warm garments and were willing to pay high prices for them. Wearing fur was also considered a sign of social status and prestige in European society.

By the 1500s, Europeans had greatly depleted their own fur resources and begun to look to other areas. But without knowing the territory, the animals' habits, or even how to best trap them, it was unlikely that European trappers would have been very successful at first in North America. As a result, the French, British, and Dutch were all eager to establish an active fur trade with the Indians.

Of the three powers, France developed the best relationship with the Abenaki. Fearing that large numbers of newcomers might upset the tribe, the only early French settlements in North America were those essential to the fur trade. The French also won over the Indians through the Catholic missionaries they sent to convert them. While British traders saw the Indians only as a resource to exploit, the French took a personal interest in them. French Jesuits learned the Indians' language and tried to see to their health care needs. Perhaps even more important, French missionaries promised their Abenaki converts military protection from their long time enemies—the Iroquois.

Diminishing the Iroquois's power was mutally beneficial, because the Iroquois largely traded furs with the British, France's primary competition for North American riches. The French also gave the Abenaki muskets to use against their enemies, while the British had strict rules against lending weapons to the Indians or trading guns for fur pelts. Although the Abenaki favored the French, some still traded with the British when they believed it benefited them to do so. Nevertheless, before long the Indian's value to the British sharply decreased. While at first the Abenaki had helped early British settlers fend off star-

MISSISQUOI VILLAGE AND MISSION
Swanton/Highgate

The ancient Missisquoi/Mazipskoik Abenaki village was the region's focal point into the 1760's. In 1744, Jesuits built a cabin which served into the 1790's as the first longterm Christian mission in Vermont. Speculators took much of the Abenaki land by 1798, but the Abenaki Nation of Missisquoi survived. In the 1860's, Swanton historian John Perry lamented the hasty destruction of the old village noting its antiquity and great importance to all. Nearby, the Abenakis live quietly to this day.

A PLAQUE MARKS THE SPOT OF AN EARLY JESUIT MISSION IN WHAT IS NOW VERMONT.

vation by bringing them food, white settlers eventually learned to meet their own needs. Now the situation was reversed as the Indians became increasingly dependent on the British who were actively pushing the French out of the area.

Instead of making what they needed as in the past, the Abenaki eagerly looked forward to trading their pelts for British-manufactured iron axes, knives, and fishhooks. The Indians had also become accustomed to using imported brass to fashion their arrowheads and needles as well as prespun cloth for garments and other coverings.

Their predicament worsened as the fur trade significantly declined over the years. Heavy hunting severely depleted the region's beaver supply, and these animals were slow to reproduce. By 1665, the fur trade had sharply waned. And the only thing the Indians had left that the British wanted was their land. Unfortunately in some cases, acquisition of Abenaki land wasn't difficult. The Abenaki still wanted European goods, so the British extended credit to them, providing that the Indians put up their land for *collateral.* When the Abenaki were unable to pay for the items with animal skins, the British seized their land.

Other factors also played havoc with the Abenaki's well being. Between 1616 and 1617 a devastating *epidemic* swept the area, drastically reducing the Indian population. Though the precise disease was not identified, it was one that the whites brought from Europe to North America, and therefore might have been cholera, dysentery, scarlet fever, typhus, or whooping cough.

Tragically, these diseases were especially lethal to American Indians. Unexposed to these illnesses, the Indians had no *immunity* to them. As a result, they were more likely to be stricken and less likely to survive. The Abenaki suffered further when in 1633 small

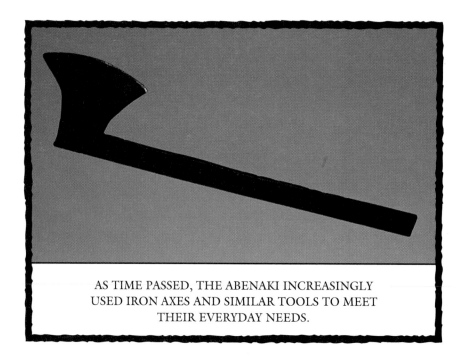

AS TIME PASSED, THE ABENAKI INCREASINGLY
USED IRON AXES AND SIMILAR TOOLS TO MEET
THEIR EVERYDAY NEEDS.

pox swept the region. While thousands of Indians died, only two white settlers perished. Besides epidemics, the American Indians also faced the chronic diseases, such as tuberculosis, brought by the Europeans. Dealing with both sickness and sharply reduced numbers, it became increasingly difficult for the Abenaki and other tribes to resist the encroaching British.

To their further disadvantage, the Abenaki were among the American Indians who became caught up in the struggle between England and France for

North American dominance. Because the Abenaki always felt closer to the French, a number of Abenaki groups fought alongside them in battles against the British. The Abenaki's anti-British sentiments were further fueled by the British military alliance with the Iroquois.

The Abenaki also conducted their own raids against the British. In time, this fighting increased in response to the brutal British attacks on Abenaki villages. Among the American Indians who distinguished themselves in the struggle was a Western Abenaki named Grey Lock. Grey Lock began a series of raids against the British in August 1723, and before long became a legendary fighter. Although the British built Fort Dummer in 1724 to shield their frontier settlers against his attacks, Grey Lock's lightening swift raids continued successfully. Many times the British sent out scouting parties to capture him, but they never succeeded.

The ongoing warfare between the Abenaki and the British continued from about 1675 to the 1760s, with only a few brief peaceful periods. In the end, there were serious losses on both sides. Although the Abenaki had won numerous battles, their resources were depleted after decades of fighting. Scores of young Abenaki men died in battle, while a continuing stream of English soldiers and settlers flooded Indian

THIS CARVING OF CHIEF GREY LOCK STANDS AS A
TRIBUTE TO THE BRAVE ABENAKI LEADER. GREY LOCK WAS
BOTH FEARED AND RESPECTED BY HIS BRITISH ENEMIES.

lands. Exhausted by the struggle, some of the remaining Abenaki fled north. They resettled in Canada where they were warmly welcomed by other Abenaki and French missionaries. Others stayed where they were, trying to carry on their lives as in the past.

In many ways this was impossible to do. At the start of the American Revolution the Abenaki once again found themselves living in a battle zone. Some Abenaki (largely those in Canada) sided with the British, while others fought valiantly for the colonists. Still other Abenaki tried to remain neutral. As the fighting drew near, they left their villages and set up temporary camps in the outlying areas.

Regardless of the Indians' position in the American Revolution, it soon became clear that the whites wanted Abenaki lands. That was the case with the Penobscots, a group of Eastern Abenaki in Maine who fought with the colonists against the British. Despite the Briton's naval superiority off the coast of Maine, the Penobscots held the interior area for the rebels. Their assistance was a determining factor in the territory assigned to the United States in the 1783 peace treaty.

The valued assistance of these Eastern Abenaki, however, was quickly forgotten after the colonists' victory. White-owned and -operated lumber companies had grown especially desirous of the Abenaki's rich timber lands. And as a result, the Penobscots, as well as other area Indians, were forced to surrender increasing amounts of their territory to the newcomers.

In other areas, Western Abenaki faced a similar dilemma. Yet despite the efforts of settlers to drive them out, many of these American Indians found ways to keep their land or at least remain in the vicinity. Some did so by continually moving from camp to camp, while living off the land. Knowing the terrain well allowed others to remain in remote spots, such as rarely traveled swamp areas. Although they were in contact with other Indians, they were rarely seen by whites.

When anti-Indian sentiment ran high, still other Western Abenaki survived by trying to blend in with the surrounding settlers. They dressed like the settlers, used similar tools, and were careful to speak only English or French.

Even though they may have had to temporarily conceal their Indian heritage, many of these American Indians never forgot who they were. They eventually began to reestablish Abenaki communities. One such enclave sprang up in the Back Bay area of Swanton, Vermont. And when it was safe to do so, they continued the ancient rituals and traditions that were distinctly Abenaki.

TO SURVIVE AT TIMES SMALL GROUPS OF
WESTERN ABENAKI HAD TO CONCEAL THEM-
SELVES IN WOODED SWAMP AREAS LIKE THIS ONE.

REVIVAL

In time, the Abenaki were once again free to assert themselves. During the 1960s and 1970s, they, along with numerous other American Indian groups in the United States and Canada, demanded universal recognition of who they were as well as full restoration of their rights.

In Quebec and Becanor, Canada, Abenaki took important steps to continue their heritage and enhance their status as a people. These Indians established a cultural center as well as a corporation to provide job opportunities and sales outlets for Abenaki crafts workers. The Abenaki Museum and the annual summer festival hosted by the Abenaki of Odanak, Quebec, further serve to celebrate who they are.

MINDFUL OF THEIR HERITAGE AS THEY SIT
OUTSIDE A TRADING POST, THESE ABENAKI GIRLS
REPRESENT THEIR PEOPLE'S FUTURE.

In the United States, the Eastern Abenaki Penobscots along with some other Maine Indians sought to reclaim lands wrongfully taken from them. Although the Indians weren't taken seriously at first, they eventually filed a federal court suit claiming as their own two-thirds of what is presently known as Maine.

The Indians argued that treaties were wrongfully broken and that the Federal Trade and Non-Intercourse Act of 1790 had been violated. This act specified that Indian lands could not be transferred to non-Indians without Congressional approval. The case was settled out of court after an acceptable settlement had been worked out between the Indians and the U.S. government. The final agreement was signed by President Jimmy Carter on October 10, 1980, and went into effect December 12th of that year. Since the settlement, the Penobscots have purchased several additional land tracts in Maine. The group's present land holdings now exceed 150,000 acres (60,700 ha).

Western Abenaki in Vermont have also begun a number of projects to enhance their people's well being and pride in being American Indians. These include a self-help association, an Indian Education Program, a scholarship fund, a women's support group, and an Abenaki children's dance troupe. Their

Family and Community History Project assists Abenaki families in locating lost relatives and supports traditional ties within and between Abenaki families.

These American Indians have also waged a legal battle for the *aboriginal title* to their ancestral territory, the area now northwest Vermont. The term refers to the right of American Indians to use and occupy what has been Indian land "from time immemorial." Legal recognition of the Western Abenaki's claim to the aboriginal title would mean that the Western Abenaki would have the same rights their ancestors had to hunt, fish, and travel on these lands. Under these conditions the Abenaki could do so without obtaining state hunting and fishing licenses.

The Abenaki had challenged the state's ownership of the property through a 1987 "fish-in" on Vermont's Missisquoi River. At that time thirty-six American Indians were arrested for fishing without state licenses. It looked as if the Abenaki would win in their struggle when in 1989 Judge Joseph Wolchik of the District Court in St. Albans upheld the Indians' right to do so. This lower court decision was overturned, however, by the Vermont Supreme Court on June 12, 1992. According to the Supreme Court, Abenaki claims to the area have been extinguished "by the increasing weight of history." Protesting the

CONSCIOUS OF PRESERVING THE ENVIRONMENT,
HERE ABENAKI REMOVE LITTER FROM A RIVER.

decision, the Abenaki questioned "how the Vermont Supreme Court could weigh 200 years of white history against over 10,000 years of Abenaki history and decide that the 200 years of white history weighs more." They view the state Supreme Court ruling as just another "attempt to excuse what their people (the whites) have done to our land and our people since they got here."

The Indians further argued that because they are a sovereign (independent) Indian nation, the Vermont Supreme Court does not have jurisdiction over them. They have also emphasized that the legal system of their oppressors cannot be objective and fair in making decisions regarding Indian territorial rights.

Despite the legal setback, the Western Abenaki have vowed to continue the struggle for their rights. This could take the form of further legal action, protest demonstrations, and even buying land sites that have been historically important to their people. The first such purchase was of the Abenaki's ancient healing springs in Brunswick, Vermont. These springs have been used by the Abenaki both in ancient and modern times "for healing of the body and spirit."

The Western Abenaki hope to one day gain federal recognition as an American Indian tribe, as the

Eastern Abenaki of Maine have done. Although they have been denied this status in the past, the Western Abenaki intend to reapply for it. The problem they face is that obtaining federal recognition requires that they prove that their tribe continually remained in Vermont through the centuries. This has been a challenge for the group because of the nature of their history. An Abenaki spokesperson described their plight this way: "While many of our ancestors were forced to go underground and hide their Abenaki identity for the sake of survival, we have never stopped living from the land or taking care of it."

Regardless of the obstacles ahead, these American Indians are determined to ensure the survival of their ancestral land and culture. They have stated, "We of the Abenaki Nation would like to tell the public that we are still here. Our ancestors never left this land and neither will our children. We are a sovereign nation and we will not stop fishing, hunting, and traveling on our land."

Although they have already achieved a great deal, the Abenaki struggle continues today.

GLOSSARY

Aboriginal title The right of present-day American Indians to use the land of their ancestors

Breechclout A piece of tanned animal skin or cloth worn around the hips and thighs

Collateral Land or something else of value put up as a guarantee that a loan will be repaid

Epidemic A widespread disease affecting many people

Fast To purposely go without food for a period of time

Immunity Body's ability to protect itself against disease

Shaman An American Indian healer believed to have spiritual powers

Smoke A process through which fish or meat is treated with smoke to preserve it

Vision quest An American Indian practice in which a young man, who has fasted, goes to a remote place hoping to see his guardian spirit in a dream or vision. Indians believed that a person's guardian spirit protects that individual from danger and harm.

Waterfowl A waterbird or swimming game bird

FOR FURTHER READING

Bruchac, Joseph. *Thirteen Months on a Turtle's Back: A Native American Year of Moons.* New York: Philomel Books, 1992.

Diamond, Arthur. *Smallpox and the American Indian.* San Diego: Lucent, 1991.

Freedman, Russell. *An Indian Winter.* New York: Holiday House, 1992.

Hirschfelder, Arlene, and Beverly R. Singer, eds. *Rising Voices: Writings of Young Native Americans.* New York: Scribner, 1992.

Liptak, Karen. *North American Indian Survival Skills.* New York: Franklin Watts, 1990.

Murdoch, David. *North American Indians*. New York: Knopf, 1995.

Sattler, Helen Roney. *The Earliest Americans*. New York: Clarion, 1993.

White Deer of Autumn: The Native American Book of Knowledge. Hillsboro, Ore.: Beyond Woods, 1992.

Williamson, Roy A., and Jean Girard Monroe. *First Houses: Native American Homes and Structures*. Boston: Houghton Mifflin, 1993.

Wood, Marion. *Spirits, Heroes and Hunters from North American Indian Mythology*. New York: Peter Benrick Books, 1992.

INDEX

ABOUT THE AUTHOR

Popular author Elaine Landau worked as a newspaper reporter, an editor, and a youth services librarian before becoming a full-time writer. She has written more than ninety nonfiction books for young people, including *The Sioux*, *The Hopi*, *The Cherokees*, *The Chilula*, and *The Pomo*. Ms. Landau, who has a bachelor's degree in English and journalism from New York University and a master's degree in library and information science from Pratt Institute, lives in New Jersey with her husband and son.

DISCOVERING U.S. HISTORY

World War II

1939–1945

DISCOVERING U.S. HISTORY

The New World: Prehistory–1542

Colonial America: 1543–1763

Revolutionary America: 1764–1789

Early National America: 1790–1850

The Civil War Era: 1851–1865

The New South and the Old West: 1866–1890

The Gilded Age and Progressivism: 1891–1913

World War I and the Roaring Twenties: 1914–1928

The Great Depression: 1929–1938

World War II: 1939–1945

The Cold War and Postwar America: 1946–1963

Modern America: 1964–Present